In The Cinema

Stephen Bone

Published by Playdead Press 2014

© Stephen Bone 2014

Stephen Bone has asserted his rights under the Copyright, Design and Patents Act, 1988, to be identified as the author of this work.

A CIP catalogue record for this book is available from the British Library.

ISBN 978-1-910067-24-6

Printed by CMP-UK

Playdead Press
www.playdeadpress.com

In memory of my parents

Acknowledgements due to the following: And Other Poems, Barnet Open Poetry Competition, Hinterland, How Do I Love Thee?, Ink, Sweat& Tears, Links, Londongrip, Poetry@3, Poetry Nottingham, Seam, Shotglass, Smiths Knoll, Snakeskin, The Galway Review, The Interpreter's House, The Lake, The Rialto, Yorkmix.

Stephen Bone was educated at the Arts Educational Trust in London and has since worked in television, theatre and radio. Working for some years for Radio Four.

First collection *In The Cinema* published Playdead Press 2014.

Contents

Coal Tar

Still available. A throwback
to cigarette cards and iodine.
Victory Vs. Spit and polish.

The soap, my aunt, who wasn't,
scrubbed herself with
as if she were a stain.
Her water hard and scalding.

Used to ease her father's
signet ring from her finger
on hot airtight days

and on me the time I slipped up.
I have never forgotten
the froth, the taste

or the way she set down
a tablet in the lodgers' bathroom
beside the copper taps,
like an unwritten house rule.

An orange threat.

Miss

Each morning after porridge
or sometimes something reheated
I hadn't managed, she walked me
to the bus stop.

Her hair immovably set; handbag
held like a weapon, her flint grey tweeds
worn even when it sweltered, perspiration
dampening her Yardley powder.
To cool herself she swore by tea, drunk
magma hot, the colour of creosote.

Some nights a younger woman
with her eyes would come round.
But most she spent black marking
the world pouring from her wireless.

Once not thinking I called her *Miss*
and she boiled up like milk.

Arctic Fox

For decades it must have hung -
this last relic of her vanity -
like an unwanted rescue dog
in her wardrobe's mothballed cave.
Room to breathe, the Danish furrier had said.

Burlesquely I wrap myself in its embrace,
feel an almost living warmth, dark hint
of an Arctic summer running through
the narrow head and back.

A stale whisper of its perfumed history,
returning her in Kodak colour
sipping Fernet Branca on Alpine terraces
or promenading Cunard decks. Mouth full-blown
with Victory Red; amber eyes like set traps.

Windfall

I watch the shallow rise
and fall of your chest
as you sip thimblefuls
of air. Listen to the clock
move on the day, the tea trolley
come and go. I tidy your bottles,
touch your face. Tidy them again.
I pour water, wind your watch.
Open the blind; a windfall
of sunlight drops around your bed.
I gather it up.

78s

Emptying your loft
I came across them
behind the gramophone.
The size of dinner plates
and just as breakable.

Took each one in turn
from its grey cardboard cover
and lowered the wind-up's
heavy snakelike arm onto
unfamiliar names -

Tino Rossi. Al Bowlly.
Mistinguett. Listened
to distant talents
scratched with age.
Their voices

now and then slurring
under the drag of the needle
as the turntable slowed. Like
grotesque recordings from their
deathbeds.

Until, with a few turns
of my arm – as if cranking up
a vintage car – their lungs filled
again with thirties' air. Resurrected
to the prime of your life.

Attic

The sturdy steamer trunks
scabbed with peeling labels.

The rusted rictus
of an upturned grate.

An abacus subtracting
beads onto the floor.

A blind doll. A flock
of damaged shuttlecocks.

A gramophone long retired,
Toscanini At The Met, still in place.

A Baby Belling.
A yellow beach ball

still limply holding
his father's breath.

Lamp

After they had come for you
the rooms began to follow,

first the furniture,
then the smaller things,

the convex mirror,
the Chinese prints,

until the house
had undressed

to the picture hooks
and a lamp on a timer

telling passers-by
where you're not.

Medlars

From the cupboard under your stairs
you pick one from its tray.
A sort of apple, open-ended,
on the turn.

Try, you urge, a spoon waved
like a hypnotist's chain. Reluctantly,
a child braced for medicine I open up
to be fed a scoop of decay.

Good? You ask, moist rot melting
to the cusp of sweetness. I tremble a nod
as you slough off your snakeskin boots;
coil yourself into a chair.

Story

How many
times?

Three. Four.

And still
that moment
somewhere in
the middle

tricking me
into thinking things
will turn out
alright.

Catch myself
hoping for
the alternative
ending.

The one
that ruins
the story.

In The Cinema

Your whispered
words silently
replay themselves -

don't tell me how it ends
don't spoil it for me.

Rain

Each day the mercury crept up,
the horizon smudged with August heat,

our shirts mapped with sweat,
baked tarmac beneath our Raleigh wheels

passing gardens foxed like old prints,
dogs lolled in them indecent on their backs,

lengths of pink unsheathed;
hose pipes coiled, unused, forbidden.

Water precious as silver we shared baths
where we stopped or dipped flannels into feeble streams;

at night our skin a layer too much
as we sprawled or tangled on sepia grass.

Set To Continue, the news stands read.
The forecast held. In part.

Landlocked

You put down
your brush.

Stand back -

a platinum sea
after rain,

a late sun rusting
the horizon, a fleck
of red sail -

and wish
your canvas
still our
window.

Unmendable

The vase we bought together
in Murano

slipped through
my careless hands

to hit the floor
with a rich percussion,

a jigsaw of glass
at our feet.

For a moment like haruspices
we studied the red remains;

then the word arrived,
reached you first;

unmendable, you said.

Inventory

The teak table,
the Chinese lamps,
brandy balloons -
always too much for me -
take freely.

The dog is mine.
But please remove
the parakeet.

And before I forget.
Help yourself to the wine
drenched evenings. Holidays.
Shared baths. First meeting.

The Rest Of Him

He went out more.
Did more.

Worked his address book
from A – Z.

Grew a beard,
mapped out his days;

took himself away
whenever he could.

The rest of him
somewhere behind.

Dawn Chorus

Shake off the night's
dark scenarios

tear yesterday from the wall
tilt your mind

towards the newly minted sun
risen like a giant florin

to the blackbird's coloratura
dew damp grass

the bakers across the street
at work for hours

with their fired ovens
floury rituals old as Genesis
recharge

yourself with strong coffee
then open your door and board

the up and running day
ready
to take you anywhere

Ode To A Deckchair

Roused
from cobwebbed hibernation,
you regain yourself, emblem
of holidays. Sun soaked
dreams of cornflower skies
and slumped ease
unfolded
with your teak bones.
A weathered veteran
brave faced to the washout
in city parks, suburban yards;
a salted sea dog,
your striped lap punching
back at the gale, robust
as the bandstand's brass
blown tunes. Far
from the pier's oily air
your true worth shown;
benign as a life boat
among the shoes
and crockery
you offer yourself,
a buoyant chance
against all odds.

Pre-Emptive

In the seafront
guest houses
a different morning
is already
set.
Upturned cups
on saucers
cereal
beside the fine cut.

As if
a piece of tomorrow
had worked its way free
or broken off.
And waits
cocksure
for the rest
to follow.

Picnic

They turn up now and then,
the photos of our picnic;

wine bottles dead on the grass,
a heatwave's emphatic shadows,

you standing on your hands,
claiming you were holding up the world;

and the other moments,
the wasp attack, the freak shower.

Have you your photos somewhere?

Willow Pattern

A patterned fence zigzags
across our path and we
can go no further into
this blue and white Orient.

Here there is no sound. No oxygen.
Is it sunup or dusk? Time has braked.
But a sense of freshness clings to the lacquer
and pagoda trees as if it had just rained.

We can only guess what cargoes are carried
in the oared boat on the milky lake.
Caskets of nephrite, perhaps, or opium pipes. Jars
of ginger and green tea. Bronze tubs of coal.

Who are the three on the footbridge
under the willow? Carp fishers, hunters
after water deer or the Imperial Guard
searching for the runaways?

His silked Majesty making offerings
in the pillared temple; sticks of sandalwood
releasing snakes of fragrant smoke. His face
furrowed as a Shar Pei with anxiety -

never to come down the steps and see
what we can see, his child and serf lover
divinely changed into soaring sapphire songbirds,
forever free. Forever unable to escape.

Sakura

The pond darkens
to its evening
pattern

of gold koi
and lilies
on black silk

but no
expensive geisha
here

just me

among
the raked white
metaphors

watching
blushed petals
fall

Fritillary

Scrap of Turkish
carpet, October leaf;

airborne
dancer riding fragrant
currents

with skip and dart;
pearled slurper

of nectaries
of ragged-robin,
bugle, self-heal,
buttercup.

Not so bad then
an inchworm life

of toil and spin,
heave and crawl

if our reward
were this.

Pedicurist

Textbook arches to calloused toes
gnarled as root ginger come my way -
scholar of the lotus foot, the hennaed sole -
to be soaked in basins of salted water. Pumiced,
clipped; anointed with lavender or bergamot.
My head bowed low to my work. A connoisseur,
hands awake to each detail.

Come bedtime, a whispered litany
of bone and muscle – *distal phalanges,*
sesamoids, flexors, extensors... smooth
on my tongue. Each word savoured. Sucked
at like a boiled sweet; as parades of slipperless
Cinderellas start to tightrope my spine.

Pork

You talked about the day
the slaughter man was summoned.
The squealing panic. Stun gun. Blades.
Wheelbarrow filled with slops of red and blue;
lungs and spinal cord fed to the cats.

The farmhand who put his lips
to the sow's limp bladder,
made a balloon
then hung it in a tree.

Later you confessed
the best you had ever eaten
though you had wanted it
the worst.

Red

it's the emergency's
pulsing flash

and daubed warning
across the derelict

the emphatic stop
glowing invite

the gape of the scream
the rolled out pomp

it's the shepherd's
delight or dismay

a stain of poppies
the sindoor dot

a clown's greasepainted
ear to ear

a spurt of ketchup
the bull's eye shot

clings to cardinals
fills the communion cup

decorates the valentine
flows through

the tributaries
of the heart

plushly blooms
beneath the knife

give me another colour
you can't live without

Silence

it's the lake to float your thoughts on
the stave waiting for a swarm of notes

buzzes with prayer in holy places
occupies deep space

it's the lock-up for secrets
counterpart of night

the hallmarked moment
pregnant pause

it's the command of libraries
wisdom of the unsaid

punctuates the argument
brings home the point

it's the target to shatter with gunshot
tension before the result

spokesman for loss
that unmistakable voice

A New Kind Of Rain

He phoned
his grandmother
to fetch him early.
Rained off, he sulked,
not hearing the flatness
in her voice, the intake
of breath, on the edge
of saying something
but didn't.

Her eyes were red
and she was wearing
more powder than usual.
He could smell its rose-like
scent as she gently pulled
him to her, before
he heard the slow, quiet
sentences...

On the journey home
he sat silently beside her,
digging a fingernail deep
into his thumb;
watching the wipers
frantic
to keep up
with a new kind
of rain.

Mind Reader

Across the coffee cups
he touches a face
he doesn't see. Traces
the outline of lips,
eyelids; fingertips
the forehead. Smiles.
As if reading his lover's
thoughts in Braille.

Doreen's Bath

Holding her orange ice,
Doreen lowers herself into water
flushed with synthetic rose.
And with pink nails unwraps her treat.

Takes cautious bites -
to avoid its shock -
until all that's left
is the burn in her mouth.

Then closing turquoise
shadowed eyes
sinks back further into
her bath.

A tiny plank
floating like flotsam;
the distant stop start
of *Greensleeves* outside.

Squatter

Her emptiness
like damp flats
he could
smell at once.
Decided
to take
his chance;
picked open
her locks
and housed
himself
in the four
chambers
of her heart.

Vinyl

Times
he puts them
on again,

takes each
from its
sleeve

wipes
away the dust
with a micro cloth,

then stacks
them high
and listens

to the first
black disc
drop,

the familiar
static
across the tracks,

the needle
sticking
here and there.

Ash

In extreme age
a girl would come
to cut his hair -
wisps that grew
like spun sugar
on a head otherwise
smooth and pink
as on his birthday.

A towel
around his shoulders,
her scissors
flashing
like a heliograph
he would sit by
the open fire;

watch logs
bubble resin,
listen
to their spit
and whine -

white hair
falling
from him
like ash.

Dragon

In black ink I uncoiled,
outstretched my wings
across the canvas of your back.

Made inseparable
with a needle's sting; a bond
of blood.

And though we can never come,
face to face, in mirrors we meet.
Where from over your white shoulder

you catch the promise
in the red dot of my eye -

the day I leave you
is the day I breathe fire.

Ice Cream

You made three flavours,
lemon, pistachio, vanilla,

juiced fragrant fruit, pestled
nuts, scraped seeds

from Madagascan pods,
whisked egg whites

to the brink of stiffness,
folded in

thick supple cream,
plump yolks, golden sugar.

For your return, you said;
a month of numbered rooms ahead,

a countdown of days
to prizing off

plastic lids, a release
of Arctic breath,

the real thing
melting on my tongue.

Private View

From their frayed album
a stray negative
falls out

I pick it off
the carpet

and like an x-ray
to be examined
hold it to the light

instantly
a smoky flashback
appears

her gown
and lilies
blackened

as if by the rage
of his white heat

a dark dead sky
above the spire

a fall
of charred stars
and horseshoes
at their feet

A Study In Sepia

Ten years before,
perhaps he walked
mud caked miles
to take the shilling,

nothing on him
but fourteen years,
a bag of apples, a rural drawl.
But here

in this sepia noon
he's made his mark astride
his plaited mare; twirled
topiary of moustache

bayonet sharp, stare
square faced to the lens appraising
a world he'll put to rights
with cut and thrust. Then

to lord it in Jaipur
a fanned and rickshawed wife;
sons of the Empire born in the foothills
away from heat and dust;

later still dank Aldershot,
marrow growing, pale ale,
rain forest and savanna baring
incisors on the Sunday parlour floor,

where hair frosted with age
he's laid out: full regalia, medal glint,
ceremonial sword, a sentry in his box,
upholder of the peace.

Tobacco

We were there
stood beside
his bed,
moments before
his heart
let him go;
listened hard
to catch the word
carried on his
closing breath.
Tobacco,
we thought
we heard him
say -
as if remembering
something
he mustn't
forget.

Camera Obscura

In a room
darkened with black blinds
today is projected onto
the screen below us.
Downland, town and sea appear,
clouds and juggernauts pass;
a couple follow a track
leading deeper into
their story and a white
horse canters
in its windswept field.

Later, walking from the tower,
becoming part of these things,
it feels like leaving
the cinema -
but in reverse.

Final Flight

Sue didn't want
her ashes to be scattered
in her native county or
from a special hill
or over the sea – although
she loved the sea – her instructions
were plain, *mixed with gunpowder
and packed into rockets.* An explosive
expert – whose company usually disposes
of live munitions for the Ministry of Defence -
was called in to make them.
All ten.

Firing them by remote
control her daughters watched
as the rockets soared
deep into the night
before releasing Sue
in a burst
of stars.

Voice-Over

We were taken onto
the terrace that day.
We often were if
the weather held.

You can see us all
breathing deeply;
as if the Margate air
could rinse us clean.

I'm third on the right.
A nurse flickering
around my iron framed
bed.

My archived
stare
travelling across
a century to reach you.